BEFRIENDING YOUR PARAKEET

A Step by Step Guide to taking absolute care of Your Parakeet

Catherine Lucas

TABLE OF CONTENT

Chapter One

Introduction
Everything You Need to Know About Your New Parakeet

Though they are common household pets, how much do you actually know about these lovely birds? You will be more equipped to ensure that your new parakeet leads a long, fulfilling life if you are more knowledgeable about it.

The Information You Should Know About Your Parakeet

Owning a parakeet may be highly gratifying, and they make wonderful companions. But in order to give them a comfortable and healthy life and build a strong owner-parakeet link you can both enjoy, it's critical to comprehend how to suit their wants.

• Personality

Due to their sociable nature, parakeets demand a lot of company. A parakeet might not be the best companion if you spend a lot of time away from home, whether it be for business or travel, or you could want to acquire more than one bird so they can keep each other company. Place the bird's cage so that it can see and hear you clearly, and chat to the bird while doing so. They will respond favorably to your encounters since they are curious.

- Lifespan

Getting a parakeet can be a serious commitment because, depending on their precise species, general health, and living conditions, these birds can live for 10 to 25 years or longer. Since children may grow up and leave for college, leaving their parakeet behind, and because older parrot owners may wish to make sure their birds can be cared for if they are unable to do so themselves, parakeets are not always the best pets for young children.

- Intelligence

Because they are intelligent birds, parakeets require enough mental engagement to prevent boredom and stress. Put a variety of perches and toys in their cage, especially bells, mirrors, and objects with unusual colors and patterns that the birds will find fascinating. Training sessions can help parakeets become more bonded to their human flock by teaching them tricks.

• Space parakeets require enough room to exercise, roost, and to avoid feeling cramped or confined. The size of the cage should be as big as your budget will allow, and the bars should have a good climbing surface that the birds cannot use to get stuck or escape. Place the cage next to where people are so that the birds may interact with you, but avoid putting it in the kitchen because the smells from cooking can be harmful to birds.

Why Exercise Parakeets will purposefully climb on their cage and perches since even caged birds need to be adequately exercised. They should have plenty of opportunity to run or walk around outside their cage, and chewing and climbing activities will keep their bills and talons in excellent condition. They will also require time to safely and securely practice using their flight muscles if their wings are not adjusted.

• Diet

In order to give adequate, balanced nutrition, parakeets require a diversified diet. The fundamental nutrition in pellets, which are sold in pet stores, is good, but for even better nutrition and to keep the bird interested in its food, seed, fruit, and vegetables should be added. Your parakeet should constantly have access to fresh water.

• Vocalizations

Parakeets sing, chirp, and even squawk like pet birds, which can make them noisy. They can mimic well, and certain species may even pick up new words or phrases. They might sing along with the music or answer you when you speak. A parakeet might not be the ideal pet if you desire a quiet companion.

• Temperature Parakeets can usually tolerate most indoor temperatures, but if you have an extremely hot or extremely cold environment, the birds may suffer. Avoid placing their cage next to windows or vents, or anywhere that will expose them to constant drafts or direct sunlight. Your bird will be more comfortable if the cage has a roosting box for shade and cover.

• Health You will need to take care of your parakeet's medical requirements, and while these birds are typically in good health, it's crucial to be alert of any symptoms of disease or suffering. Keep an eye out for changes in their hunger, examine their excrement for coloring or consistency issues, and take note of any changes in their energy level or behavior that might be problematic. Make sure you are aware of the location of the closest avian veterinarian so that you can contact them in case of an emergency or for routine exams.

If you're up for the challenge, a parakeet can make a good pet. You'll be prepared to raise your own flock of these birds once you have a basic understanding of them.

Chapter two

Choosing a Parakeet

Birds need commitment and care.

Are parakeets suitable as pets for all people? Not quite. This might not be the best time to take on this task if you don't have enough time to attend to their demands. You need to devote a lot of time and energy to caring for a parakeet, and you also need to set aside money for it. The process of learning how to care for parakeets is likewise a learning curve. Getting a pair of parakeets is a long-term commitment since, in case you didn't know, they can live for up to ten years. Parakeet birds can live for up to 15 years on occasion.

Did you know there are more than 100 different varieties of parakeets worldwide?

The budgerigar, a native of Australia, is the most typical variety of parakeet. Comparatively speaking to other varieties of parakeets, budgies make low-maintenance pets.

Before choosing a new type, find out how much a parakeet costs at your neighborhood pet store or breeders. The more expensive they are, the rarer they are.

Purchasing a pet parrot from a reputable pet retailer, like Petco or Petsmart, will spare you from having to later treat your parakeets for a variety of ailments.

Make sure the breeder you select has a great reputation for keeping healthy birds.

Choose the proper breed

find suitable birds

Make sure the parakeets you get
from the breeder or retailer
have vibrant eyes and are in
good health.

They shouldn't be filthy or
lacking in feathers. In order to
determine whether the budgies
were kept in good condition,
have a look at the housing that
they were housed in.

Additionally, the budgerigars
should be free of mites and have
no growths or deformities. Since
they spend the entire day
standing on their feet, their toes
should be in excellent condition.

If you wish to train your
budgies, it can be a good idea to

choose young birds rather than older ones.

Purchase two parakeets.

Since budgies have a very social personality, they must constantly have a friend, whether that person is a human or another bird.

It is strongly advised that you purchase two budgies rather than one because it is nearly hard for people to constantly be at their parakeet's side.

If you like, you can purchase additional budgies, but they should be from the same group. Conflicts may arise between them if they are introduced later. Together-raised parakeets frequently get along more harmoniously than those who were reared separately.

Keeping more parakeets than you can care for will need you to clean their cage more frequently, provide them with more food, and resolve any conflicts that may arise. (1) Most people can generally handle two or three persons at a time.

Chapter three

Diet

Knowing what to feed parakeets is another aspect of caring for them. People who don't do enough research on this could put their children on an unhealthy diet of only seeds or only pellets.

To thrive, parakeets require a variety diet. There are several meals that you should never give them since they run the risk of making them drunk or even fatal.

Toxins can also be found in some fruit seeds. Other issues include accidentally feeding them moldy nuts or feeding them human food that doesn't meet their nutritional demands and may be harmful to their health. What you need to know is listed below.

What foods consume parakeets?

What foods consume parakeets? Pellets, seeds, produce, fruits, nuts, and treats should make up a parakeet's typical diet.

While a large majority of their food should consist of seeds and pellets, they should also receive daily small amounts of fruits, vegetables, and legumes.

You can give them a variety of seeds, including safflower, groat, white sunflower, and canary seed. In order to give the nutrients of both grains and seeds, pellets that resemble seeds are frequently combined with them.

Fruits should only be given to your parakeets two or three times a week because of their somewhat high sugar content. Because they are healthier, vegetables should be consumed daily.

Banana, apricot, peach, apple (without the seeds), and fresh berries are a few examples of safe fruits. From cucumber and tomato to carrot, zucchini, and asparagus, there are many healthy veggies.

You can give parakeets modest portions of cooked beans and peas since legumes can provide a healthy quantity of protein to their diet.

noxious foods

When there is no more budgie food in the house, what should I feed a parakeet? Even while bread might be the first thing that comes to mind, it's not the ideal option.

Sandwich bread is inappropriate for parakeets since it contains several preservatives, chemicals, and even sugar.

Parakeets can be particularly poisoned by other meals. Here is a summary.

Yucca, chocolate, mushrooms, tomato stems, and leaves

Avocados, uncooked beans, raw peanuts, and

the majority of fruits' seeds and pits (including apples)

Alcohol, junk food, caffeinated drinks, and foods that might be overly sweet or salty should all be avoided.

Although the majority of fruits and vegetables consumed by people are thought to be safe and healthy, parakeets may be at risk since they may have been exposed to harmful levels of pesticides.

They might be included in the so-called "dirty dozen" list, which also includes strawberries and spinach that you could otherwise offer to budgies.

Treats

Giving gifts to your parakeets occasionally is part of budgie care.

Given that they aren't the healthiest diet option available, it is a good idea to feed your pet birds treats only sometimes.

They might contain honey, which is high in sugar, or they might have too many seeds compared to the daily suggested amount for parakeets.

Treat sticks and spray millet are two examples of safe parakeet foods.

Even mealworms can be given occasionally as a reward because they have a good amount of protein, but only in little amounts.

Fruits can be used as treats because of their sugar content, especially because you shouldn't feed your parrots more than twice or three times a week.

Therefore, rather than giving your parakeets a commercial treat, try finding a fruit that they enjoy.

Water

Budgies must always have access to clean water if they want to remain healthy. This means that you need at least once a day change the water for your pet birds.

Since bird feces can accidentally fall into a little dish if you do not use a waterer, you may need to clean it three to four times daily.

In contrast, if you get a waterer, you can be confident that the water will remain clean up until you replace it.

Which water is risk-free? If the source of the water is known to be clean, tap water can be utilized, however many owners of pet birds claim that if the water is categorized as "hard water," it includes too many minerals. You can offer them filtered or bottled water to address this issue.

Chapter four

Caring for Your Parakeet

It's crucial to give your budgie pair the ideal home for their safety, wellbeing, and health. Your parakeets will spend the most of their time in their cage, so make it as large as you can.

Place the cage in a room that is safe, warm, and bustling, but keep it away from the window because budgies can easily become too hot or cold.

You might occasionally remove your parakeets from their cages, either to take them to the veterinarian or to give them a little more freedom. Make sure they are released in a secure location where there is no chance of harm coming to them.

Cage

Your pet birds must have adequate room in the parakeet house for them to feel comfortable. A cage that is at least 18 by 14 by 22 inches can accommodate one parakeet. Get a bigger cage if you can, as it will increase your bird's comfort level.

If you purchase a pair of parakeets rather than a single bird, the size will be doubled. The cage bars need to be close together because budgies have been known to trap their bodies between the bars in the past.

Additionally, because parakeets use their beaks to climb up the bars of the cage, it must be built of safe materials. Zinc and lead are both harmful to birds, therefore you would never want your pet birds to swallow either of them by accident.

Additionally, bamboo cages are not a wise choice because parakeets have been known to nibble through them and escape.

cage adornments

A few accessories are essential for standard or fancy parakeet care, while others are optional.

At least three perches for your bird to stand on, a swing (which is like a perch but moves and gives your bird entertainment), two metal food bowls, one or two waterers, and a cuttlebone are all necessary.

• Bedding

You might think about purchasing a birdcage skirt if you want to maintain your birdcage as spotless as possible. With the tray easily removable for cleaning, this will at least keep some of the bedding and waste inside the cage.

Additionally, a coconut ladder hut home can be a terrific addition because it offers a secure hiding spot for your budgies to go when they need to rest and is also quite entertaining due to the stairs.

Make sure all of the accessories you purchase, regardless of their variety or type, are created from substances that are advertised as being safe for parakeets.

Toys

Understanding that parakeets might become bored if they don't have access to entertainment is another important aspect of learning how to care for them.

But which kinds of toys do budgies prefer? Think about your budgie's social tendencies while choosing toys for them. Add a mirror to the budgie's living space to make it a companion if you can only keep one. A plastic budgerigar that you can attach to a perch or the cage bars is another option.

Birds can see the entire color spectrum and even hues that humans cannot see, so choose toys that are as vivid as possible.

To ensure that your budgies never get tired of their toys, rotate or swap out the toys every so often.

Chapter five

Health Indicators of an Animal's Well-Being

Parakeets in excellent health have a healthy appetite, especially in the morning. If the bird starts to lose its appetite, there may be a health problem. Budgies are also acrobatic and lively; they don't stay still or peaceful for very long.

Every day, a healthy parakeet will spend some time grooming both themselves and their mate. Their feathers must be in good condition, smooth, and organized, and none of them may be missing. The grooming routine of a healthy budgie shouldn't change.

You should keep a check on your budgie's claws and feet because they are susceptible to numerous ailments. Their claws shouldn't be too lengthy and they should be clean and free of encrustation.

You should be aware that the parakeet's physiological temperature ranges from 102 to 112 degrees Fahrenheit.

Just like other animals, birds can get a fever, so if you find that your pet budgie is unresponsive and overheats when you hold it, it may be ill.

Here are a few more indications that a parakeet is healthy.

• A straight flight

• A strong and complete beak; a waxy cere;

• Firm dander

medical needs

Do parakeets require veterinary care? Indeed, and frequently. It is necessary to clip a parakeet's wings and nails to facilitate taming. Depending on how quickly they develop, you should trim your pet bird's nails every one to two months.

However, a veterinarian should handle both of these tasks rather than the pet owner (7)

Because budgies are little birds with little blood in their bodies, this is the case. There is a danger that you won't be able to stop a hemorrhage if you try to trim your parakeet's nails or wings by yourself.

There are breeders that are accustomed to doing this on their own without a veterinarian's help, but they were initially given instructions by a veterinary professional.

Simply ask your veterinarian for instructions if you feel confident in your ability to do so.

common ailments

The ailments that mostly affect parakeets are the most crucial parakeets information you should be aware of. By being aware of the symptoms, you can avoid them in the future.

The following are the most typical health issues that a parakeet or your pair of budgies may encounter:

Diarrhea, mites, feather plucking, and chlamydia

Parakeet chlamydiosis is a contagious illness that can be spread from an affected bird to a healthy one. Appetite loss, green feces, conjunctivitis, and nasal discharge are its hallmarks.

Feather plucking may be a symptom that your parakeets' diet is deficient in key nutrients, such as minerals, or it may be the result of boredom.

When the budgies eat something that upsets their stomach, they may experience diarrhea. However, food poisoning is another possibility.

Some parakeets living in pet stores under filthy conditions may frequently get mite infestations. The budgie in question would have white deposits, mostly on its legs and feet but occasionally even on its beak or eyes.

Please seek veterinary attention in each of these scenarios.

A red flag

Knowing when to take your parakeet to the doctor will stop

any health concern from getting worse when it comes to parakeet care. Here are several indicators that your budgies may not be feeling well and that you should take them to the vet as soon as possible.

Runny feces, green feces, fluffed or soiled feathers, coughing or respiratory difficulty, enlarged beak, absence of a grooming regimen, avoiding sitting on a perch, lack of food, red or swollen eyes, white deposits around the legs and feet, lack of appetite, red or swollen eyes.

Take your parakeets to the vet as soon as you can if you observe any of these symptoms in them.

Upkeep

Once you have acquired all of the necessary supplies for your parakeet pair, your work as their caregiver is not finished. Your duty should include a significant portion of maintenance, which might include everything from routine trips to the veterinarian to cleaning the birds' cages.

It's crucial to keep your budgies' living space clean and fresh because doing so can help them stay healthy. Like those of any other birds or mammals, their droppings contain bacteria and other pathogens.

cleaning of cages

It is false if you have seen parakeet material that says you should clean your pet birds' cage once every few weeks or even less frequently.

A non-toxic disinfectant must be used to wipe down their home after cleaning it with pet-friendly detergent at least once a week.

After cleaning the cage, give it another brush to get rid of any remaining disinfectant residue.

The waterers or food bowls must be cleaned in the same manner as the rest of the accessories. Even the toys must be cleaned once every week or every two weeks because they can also become filthy.

Grooming

Every pet parakeet has to be groomed occasionally, but if you've never done it before, it's a good idea to ask your veterinarian to show you how.

You will require some nail clippers, styptic powder, and a pair of sharp scissors for the jobs once you have mastered how to do it yourself.

Nail trimming and wing trimming are examples of budgie grooming. Today's perches, thankfully, allow for the filing down of the nails, so you might not even need to clip their nails at all.

Because trimming the wings is significantly more difficult and should be left to a professional if you have no prior experience,

Once the birds are able to fly, it must be carried out. Wing trimming typically requires two individuals, one of whom will handle the budgie and the other will perform the trimming.

Food should be combined.

Parakeets can become tired with eating the same food every day in the same way that people might.

You should occasionally switch things up to avoid getting bored, but you can also use this technique to make sure that your budgies are getting all the necessary nutrients.

While seeds and pellets should be the foundation of your budgie's food, it's also a good idea to supplement it once a week with cuttlebones, fresh fruit and vegetables, and mineral blocks.

You can give cooked legumes to your parakeets once every few days to prevent any protein shortages. The same is true for fruits, which should only be consumed once every three to four days due to their high sugar content.

Avoid always eating the same types of sweets, fruits, or vegetables. Budgies enjoy trying new things, and they will enjoy the diversity as long as you are serving them safe food.

toy assortment

You'll also need to give your birds a range of toys once you learn how to take care of a parakeet.

On websites like Chewy.com, you can purchase a sizable set, some of which include dozens of different toys for your birds to play with.

Ladders are a favorite for some, swings or toys with shiny bells or beads are preferred by others, but some birds favor fun toys like shredders.

It's a good idea to test out the toys in a set if it includes 15 or 20 of them to determine which ones your budgies prefer.

Establish a plan whereby you introduce one or two new toys to their cage every few days to prevent them from getting bored with any of them.

go to the vet

Do parakeets require veterinary care? It might be a good idea to visit the vet with your new pair as soon as you get it if you're new to caring for budgies.

The veterinarian will inspect the birds, determine whether they are healthy, and provide you with critical details that you might not be able to access online.

Regarding routine visits, you might need to bring your parakeets in for wing and nail trimming.

However, not all parakeet parents do this, so it will be one less worry if you choose a perch that files their nails.

You will need to take your parakeets to the vet once every few months for grooming requirements.

Chapter seven

Handling

Socialize

It takes some time and effort to socialize a parakeet, and the optimum time to start is when the bird is still a youngster. The budgie must constantly interact with new people, things, and environments.

Babies are when budgies learn the most. The parakeet can learn as much as they possibly can from their living surroundings since their minds start an imprinting process. During the first year of their lives, this takes place.

A parakeet is a gregarious bird, and as such, it cannot endure prolonged isolation. The bird will suffer if it doesn't engage with anyone, whether it's the pet parent or another budgie.

The following advice will help your budgie parakeet socialize.

-

When they are young, start feeding a variety of foods. Move the cage around the house so they can become used to diverse environments.

Every morning and every evening, or whenever you have some free time, talk to your parrots. Expose your parakeet to a variety of toys and obstacles, especially when you're away from home.

Allow them to occasionally leave their cage.

Every owner of a pet bird will occasionally feel tempted to let their parakeets out of the cage.

But when that occurs, it's crucial to know how to take care of parakeets.

Only secure spaces where there is no possibility of escape should be allowed for birds to soar.

Make sure there are no open windows or doors in the room you let your pet birds fly into as they can be injured by a variety of objects both within and outside the home.

Here are some additional guidelines for letting your parakeets fly around the house: • Make sure there are no other pets (cats or dogs) in the room; • Remove any plants that could be toxic if consumed by your budgies; • Turn off any fans; • Remove the blinds as a parakeet can get stuck or tangled into them; • Don't leave any closets or drawers open that might make it difficult for the parakeet to escape; •

teach them to communicate

The process of teaching your parakeets to converse can be difficult and time-consuming. It calls for some endurance.

Make sure your budgies aren't otherwise preoccupied or anxious, and cultivate a quiet environment. Make that the birds are at ease.

Since the birds are well-rested in the morning, teaching budgies to speak is best done then. Following are some steps:

Start by using a single, straightforward word (such as their name). Reward your parakeet by giving it a favorite treat and verbal praise.

Don't overdo it; a daily study session of 30 minutes is typically plenty. Speak with excitement. Gradually advance from easy words to more difficult ones, then to phrases.

Some parakeets can be trained to speak, but not all of them. It depends on the bird and the age at which you adopted it. Maintain reasonable expectations, but never give up. Practice makes perfect.

Sleeping

Parakeets make convenient pets because they typically sleep for 10 to 12 hours each day. The majority of this occurs at night.

You can drape a cloth over the cage to make it a secure space for your budgies so that they can sleep soundly.

If you do this, though, you must make sure that there is still adequate air entering the cage and that it is ventilated properly.

If your parrots have a habit of being very noisy at night, covering the cage usually stops the problem and encourages the parrots to fall asleep.

Regarding a parakeet's sleeping habits, you might also observe them during the day.

For instance, they frequently doze off by simply closing their eyes, although they occasionally sit on one foot to rest the other.

Others have the option of doing so.

How can you tell if your parakeets are content and well-being?

As soon as you start keeping budgies as pets, you'll notice how active they are. Consequently, a content parakeet will constantly be active, whether flying, chewing, playing, or climbing on various perches inside the cage. If you have a couple, they will converse with one another rather frequently as well.

In good health, parakeets also produce a variety of joyful noises, such as chirping, whistling, and even outright singing. Additionally, they graze on food all day long and occasionally even in between play periods.

An unwell parakeet will appear sad and exhibit several changes, including lethargy, a drop in appetite, listlessness, vocalizations from a normally quiet bird, and a poor overall appearance.

You might observe variations in the droppings of sick parakeets, alterations in the appearance of their feet and beaks, or ruffled, disorganized, or filthy feathers. Budgies that are happy and healthy groom themselves and their pair; hence, a lack of grooming behavior indicates that something is amiss.

Chapter Eight

How to Teach a Parakeet to Finger Train in Less Than Two Days

Over the years, I've finger-trained a lot of parakeets, and I enjoy sharing training advice with others.

Parakeet finger training is a rather simple process. If you have several birds, train one at a time rather than attempting to train them all at once. Give each bird its own attention each day.

The active tiny birds known as parakeets, often called budgerigars or "budgies," are quick to adjust to new situations and are quite gregarious. Because they don't create a lot of mess and are often simple to care for, they are frequently ideal as pets.

Training a New Parakeet by Hand

Hand-bred and kept parakeets shouldn't have any trouble becoming used to people, and by the time these budgies can fly, they are already friendly. However, parakeets that are acquired from huge commercial pet stores are frequently still wild and fearful when you obtain them because they weren't raised by hand. The post will

cover how to train a parakeet
that was acquired from a store.

Giving goodies to a timid
parakeet can help encourage it.

First, clip the wings and get
accustomed to the new
surroundings.

Before bringing a parakeet
home, have the store employee
cut both of its wing feathers to
prevent the bird from taking off
right away. Feathers regenerate

pretty quickly, but a single trim ought to be sufficient to buy you some time to train the bird. After that, you can choose whether to continue clipping the bird's feathers, which is advised if you plan to play with it outside.

It's crucial to give a parakeet time to adjust to your household when you bring it home from the pet store. It is preferable to keep it in a place that is peaceful and infrequently entered, such a guest bedroom.

Keep the parakeet in its new cage in the room and pay it a few visits during the day without opening the cage. I advise letting the bird be alone for at least a day, preferably two.

Keep your hand close to the
parakeet's foot base whether
the bird is within the cage or

not.

Although this bird is already trained, take note of the way the finger is pressing against its abdomen to get it to stand up.

Step 2: Remove the bird

Start by releasing the parakeet from its cage at the conclusion of the second day. If it emerges on its own, half the struggle is won. If not, try placing a piece of millet next to your finger and holding it there so the bird must step on it to reach the treat.

If it still doesn't appear, dim the room so you can see the parakeet, then carefully remove it from the cage using a small, light towel or a glove. Turn on the lights and place it on top of the cage.

To prevent your parakeet from flying too far, you must clip its wing feathers prior to doing this.

Be prepared for bites in Step 3

Keep some snacks close by, but set them away for the moment. Have patience with the next steps because the parakeet will probably be too afraid to feed at this point.

If you believe you might not be able to endure a parakeet bite, keep a light glove nearby. If it bites, it hurts, but it's not as bad as you might imagine. If the bird bites you, it is crucial not to jerk your hand away since doing so would teach the bird that biting you is an efficient way to make the threat (your hand) go away. Slowly stretch your finger in the direction of the parrot.

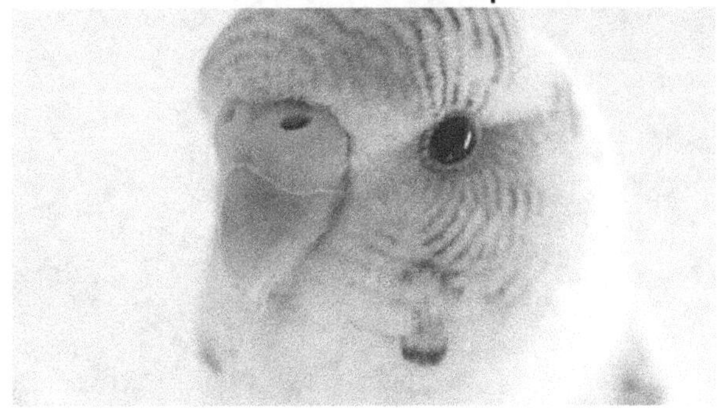

There is nowhere to go but your
hands. Be cautious though, as

nothing but your hand can be bit by this, so move slowly.

Coax the bird onto a finger in step four.

Follow the bird slowly with your finger extended if it starts to flee. The bird should land on the floor or anywhere you can reach it if it flies into the room (if you had its wing feathers trimmed).

If the bird is on the ground, sit down next to it and slowly follow it with your finger while keeping your hand close to its feet. Do not give up; the bird will be afraid and attempt to defend itself.

Try getting the bird into a situation where the only way it can escape is by jumping onto your finger or over your palm. One possibility is a corner of the room or the top of their cage.

Since the bird won't automatically jump on your finger just because you are touching it, extend your finger to the base of its feet and gently push.

Once the bird is on your finger, make an effort to get it to land on the opposite hand. Until it gets the hang of it, push against the bottoms of the feet.

Fifth Step: Switch to the Other Finger

Till the bird is on your hand, keep trying. Offer your bird some millet or another pleasant treat, but don't make it eat if it doesn't want to.

Now, using your other hand, try to persuade the bird to travel from one finger to the next. You might need to push at the bird's foot bases to get it moving. It might try to bite now, so keep your guard up and don't pull your hand away. Once more, if necessary, use a cloth glove.

Simply repeat step 4 if the bird takes off so that it is hopping from one finger to the other. Continue to provide a treat, but don't demand it.

Step 6: Continue

Shorten the workout sessions to once or twice day, 15 minutes maximum. This procedure can be repeated until the bird is willing to leave the cage.